We're Roaming in the Rainforest

An Amazon Adventure

For Connie, Lynn and Nancy: all dear friends — L. K.
Many thanks to Dr. Paul Beaver of Amazonia Expeditions for sharing
with the author his knowledge of the peoples of the rainforest.

For Simone, always in our hearts x — A. W.

Barefoot Books · 294 Banbury Road · Oxford · OX2 7ED

Barefoot Books · 2067 Massachusetts Ave · Cambridge · MA 02140

Text copyright © 2010 by Laurie Krebs. Illustrations copyright © 2010 by Anne Wilson
The moral rights of Laurie Krebs and Anne Wilson have been asserted
First published in Great Britain by Barefoot Books, Ltd and
in the United States of America by Barefoot Books, Inc in 2010
The paperback edition published in 2012

Graphic design by Louise Millar, London
Reproduction by B&P International, Hong Kong
Printed in China on 100% acid-free paper

This book was typeset in Potato Cut
The illustrations were prepared with printed papers, printing ink and acrylic paints

ISBN 978-1-84686-545-9

British Cataloguing-in-Publication Data:
a catalogue record for this book is available from the British Library

Library of Congress Cataloging-in-Publication Data is available under LCCN 2009016217

1 3 5 7 9 8 6 4 2

We're Roaming in the Rainforest

An Amazon Adventure

Written by Laurie Krebs

Illustrated by Anne Wilson

Barefoot Books
step inside a story

Rainforest sunrise. The dark fades away.
And everyone eagerly greets the new day.

"Fly," squawk the parrots,
from branches and twigs.
"We'll swoop down to breakfast
on ripe, juicy figs."

"Jump," chatter monkeys.
"Or swing if you dare."

"We'll hang by our tails and then leap through the air."

"Snooze," yawn the sloths, all ready to doze.

"We'll nap in the trees as we cling by our toes."

"Swim," gurgle pink river
dolphins with pride.
"We'll nuzzle our calves while
we swim side by side."

"Sip," murmur butterflies,
high in the sky.
"We'll lunch upon nectar
as we flutter by."

"Watch," snap the caimans, with wide-awake eyes.

"We'll offer our prey
an unwelcome surprise."

"Hide," croak the colourful poison dart frogs.
"We'll burrow down under the moss-covered logs."

"March," order leaf-cutter
ants on parade.
"We'll bury our cuttings
in the gardens we've made."

"Spin,"
hum the spiders,
perfecting a snare.

"We'll capture
our supper.
Would you like
to share?"

"S-s-scoot," hiss the gecko and lizard and snake. "We'll s-s-skitter and s-s-scamper and s-s-slither and s-s-shake."

"Crouch," growl the jaguars
as dusk closes in.
"We'll hide until dark,
when our hunt can begin."

"Hush," whisper otters
to pups in a heap.
"We'll cuddle together
till we fall asleep."

Rainforest sunset.
The moon's on the rise.
And everyone listens
to night's lullabies.

The Amazon Rainforest

There is no place in the world quite like the Amazon rainforest of South America. Most of the Amazon rainforest is in Brazil, but it also spreads into Venezuela, Colombia, Ecuador, Peru and Bolivia. It is the largest tropical rainforest on earth and home to many, many plants, animals and people. A very important part of our ecosystem, the rainforest contains trees and plants that help us breathe by changing carbon dioxide into oxygen. For this reason, the rainforest is often called the "lungs of our planet".

The Amazon River is the most extensive river system in the world. Beginning as a trickle in the Andes Mountains of Peru, it travels more than four thousand miles across Brazil to the Atlantic Ocean. Its rivers, streams and tributaries — the branches of a river — flow through Colombia, Venezuela, Ecuador, Bolivia and the three Guyanas. The Amazon River provides two-thirds of the earth's fresh water and beneath its surface live more than two thousand kinds of fish.

Nearly half a million species of plants have been recorded in the Amazon rainforest. One-fifth of the world's birds, hundreds of mammals, more than a thousand varieties of frogs and an amazing number of reptiles and insects are found there. Scientists believe even more plants and animals are yet to be discovered. People have lived in the rainforest for thousands of years, sometimes along the river, sometimes deep in the jungle. When plants, animals and people live in balance with one another, the rainforest thrives.

Caribbean Sea

VENEZUELA

COLOMBIA

GUYANA SURINAME FRENCH GUIANA

ECUADOR

The Amazon River

THE AMAZON
RAINFOREST

PERU

PACIFIC
OCEAN

BOLIVIA

ATLANTIC
OCEAN

BRAZIL

CHILE

PARAGUAY

ARGENTINA

URUGUAY

SOUTH
AMERICA

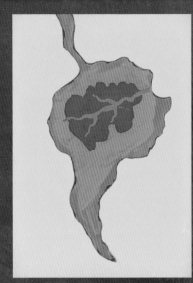

Peoples of the Peruvian Amazon Rainforest

Today most people in the Amazon area live in cities or towns. However, many indigenous — or native — tribes still dwell in the rainforest. Many live as their ancestors did, relying on the forest to provide them with food, shelter, tools and medicine. In the northern reaches of Amazonia, some groups still have little or no contact with the outside world. Most indigenous Amazonians believe that spirits live in plants and animals, so they respect all living things and try to use the forest's resources wisely.

The Matis

The Matis Indians, who practise an ancient way of life, are one of these tribes. Known as the Jaguar People, they paint their faces, tattoo their bodies and put spines from the black palm through their noses to imitate the features of a jaguar. They perform colourful rituals such as the Ceremony of Mariwin, in which the men paint their bodies black and wear red masks and green leaves. The masks represent ancestral spirits.

The Matis men are among the best hunters in the Amazon. When they hunt, they use a thirteen-foot-long blowgun and poison darts instead of the traditional bow and arrow. The Matis are a proud people who keep to themselves in order to preserve their heritage.

The Yanomami

The families in a Yanomami village live together in a great house called a shabono. Shaped like a ring, the shabono is open in the middle. Here, feasts and ceremonies take place. A thatched-roof building encircles the opening; inside, each family has its own living space. Being together in one large house protects the people from warring tribes or unwelcome strangers.

The Yanomami hunt and fish in the rainforest. They grow a nutritious root crop called cassava and a kind of banana called a plantain.

The Ribereños

The Ribereños, or River People, live at the edge of the Amazon River in small family villages. Each settlement consists of several houses built of wood which are open on three sides. The homes have watertight roofs woven from palm thatch and sit on stilts that raise them above yearly floodwaters.

Ribereños have more contact with outsiders than tribes living deep in the rainforest, so their life is a mix of old and new ways. River People depend on the forest for their food and medicine. They travel in hand-carved dugout canoes. Most follow age-old customs and believe in the spirit world, but unlike forest tribes who wear little or no clothing, the Ribereños wear T-shirts, shorts and skirts. They attend local schools, learn to read and write and prepare for jobs outside the village. Today's Ribereños are living with a foot in each world.

For the indigenous people of the Amazon, life has always centred on the well-being of the rainforest. They have lived in harmony with nature for thousands of years . . . a lesson for the world.

Conservation

Today, the human population of the rainforest has grown by leaps and bounds as business people around the world discover the Amazon's riches. Corporations are sending workers to log its trees, mine its gold and set up cattle ranches. Roads serving these industries are carved through the forest, destroying wildlife. Thousands of acres are burned to clear land for farms. Sadly, the rainforest is shrinking and many native plants and animals have disappeared forever. As people move into the area to serve the companies, local tribes, who once counted in their millions, are shrinking in number.

Scientists and conservationists are working to protect and preserve the rainforest. They are sharing new ideas to bring money to the area and provide support for the people living there. Native trees and plants are often destroyed by slash-and-burn farming, but we need to allow them to stand in order to provide an ongoing supply of nutritious nuts, oils and healing medicines. New trees are being planted and improved farming methods are being developed. Local people are trained for the tourist industry, which helps to pay for medical care and village schools. Governments are encouraged to pass laws protecting the rainforest. These efforts are helping to restore the delicate balance of this important, enchanting place.

Please contact the following organisations to find out how you can help:
    Oxfam: www.oxfam.org
    Survival International: www.survivalinternational.org
    The Woodland Trust: www.woodlandtrust.org.uk
    The Prince's Rainforests Project: www.rainforestsos.org

Creatures of the Peruvian Amazon Rainforest

The Amazon rainforest is home to many creatures, large and small.
Here are the ones pictured in this book:

Short-Tailed Parrots — Beautiful, intelligent and playful, Amazonian parrots were among the first creatures Christopher Columbus saw in the New World. They are especially noisy in the early morning and at dusk.

Spider Monkeys — Spider monkeys live in social groups called troops. They are great acrobats and can leap from a tree branch on one side of a narrow river to a branch on the other side.

Three-Toed Sloths — Sloths are slow-moving, shy mammals that spend most of their lives hanging upside down from tree branches. They sleep many hours of the day but are more active at night.

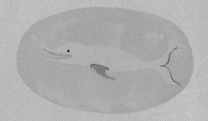

Pink River Dolphins — With flexible bodies and friendly, curious natures, pink river dolphins have been known to push drowning villagers safely ashore when their canoes have overturned.

Blue Morpho Butterflies — Tiny scales on their wings reflect light and produce the brilliant colour of the blue morpho butteflies. Ancient people thought butterflies were angels because their folded wings looked like praying hands.

Black Caimans — Meat-eating reptiles, black caimans live in freshwater areas of the rainforest. They are excellent swimmers, with webbed feet and powerful tails that propel them through the water.

Poison Dart Frogs — These colourful frogs, smaller than a thumbnail, have poisonous skin. Predators, tasting the poison, get very sick and quickly learn to leave the frogs alone.

Leaf-Cutter Ants — Leaf-cutter ants are the world's first farmers. They carry pieces of leaves to their nests and chew them into pulp. A special fungus, growing on the pulp, is their food.

Spiders — Web-weaving spiders spin sticky threads to capture insects and then paralyse them with their venom. Hunting spiders, like tarantulas, use poisonous fangs or powerful jaws to kill their prey.

Green Iguanas — One of many rainforest lizards, green iguanas grow to be six feet long. Young lizards hunt for insects and worms on the forest floor. Adults live in trees and feast mostly on plants.

Geckos — Geckos are the only lizards that have voices. Their clicking, squeaking noise sounds just like their name, "gecko". They have sticky toe pads to help them climb smooth surfaces.

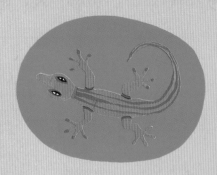

Anacondas — Anacondas, members of the boa family, are among the largest, most powerful snakes in the world. Although most baby snakes hatch from eggs, mother anacondas, like humans, give birth to living young.

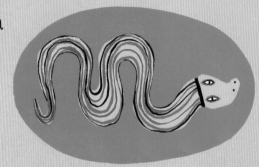

Jaguars — Jaguars are large, solitary cats that are now quite rare in the wild. Among ancient people, they were identified with royalty as symbols of power, strength and bravery in warfare.

Giant River Otters — River otter families live in mud caves along the banks of lakes and rivers. Stubby feet make the otters awkward on land but strong, flattened tails help them to be swift and agile swimmers.